FLORES

DEL

VOLCÁN

FLOWERS

FROM THE

VOLCANO

Flores del volcán

CLARIBEL ALEGRÍA

Traducción de

CAROLYN FORCHÉ

University of Pittsburgh Press

Flowers from the Volcano

CLARIBEL ALEGRÍA

Translated by
CAROLYN FORCHÉ

University of Pittsburgh Press

Published by the University of Pittsburgh Press, Pittsburgh, Pa. 15260
Feffer and Simons, Inc., London
Manufactured in the United States of America
Second Printing 1985

Library of Congress Cataloging in Publication Data

Alegría, Claribel.
  Flowers from the volcano.

  (Pitt poetry series)
  Title on added t.p.: Flores del volcán.
  Parallel text in English and Spanish.
    I. Forché, Carolyn. II. Title. III. Title: Flores
del volcán. IV. Series.
PQ7539.A47F513   1982   861   82-70893
ISBN 0-8229-3469-8   AACR2
ISBN 0-8229-5344-7 (pbk.)

"In Salvador, Death" from *Song of Protest* by Pablo Neruda. Translated by Miguel Algarín. English translation Copyright © 1976 by Miguel Algarín. Reprinted by permission of William Morrow & Company.

Some of the translations in this book originally appeared in *The Chowder Review*.

*The publication of this book is supported by grants
from the National Endowment for the Arts
in Washington, D.C., a Federal agency,
and the Pennsylvania Council on the Arts.*

for Bud Flakoll

In Salvador, Death

In Salvador, death still patrols.
The blood of dead peasants
has not dried, time does not dry it,
rain does not erase it from the roads.
Fifteen hundred were machine-gunned.
Martinez was the assassin's name.
Since then a bloody flavor soaks
the land, the bread and wine in Salvador.

—Pablo Neruda

ÍNDICES

CONTENTS

PREFACE:
With Tears, with Fingernails and Coal

"I have no *fusil* [rifle] in my hand, but only my testimony." Her hands sculpt her language as she speaks. The late sun dissolves in the Mediterranean, the hour's bells drop down the terraces of Mallorca. She moves into another of her memories.

"I was attending a conference of writers and intellectuals. We Latin Americans were sitting around our table and it seems that there was a package addressed to us. It was casually tossed from one mailboy to another. The one who caught it was killed. The other was injured in the explosion. Months later, in another part of the world, I was asked what I would have done if we had been issued rifles. I explained that I could not take up the gun, that I would not be good with a gun. I would have asked for bandages and medicines instead—this is one thing I know how to use. The other is the word."

The ink of memory washed in blood, clouds that are wrapped around the open wounds of the *Cordillera.* Claribel Alegría is a poet who has called herself a cemetery, willing to provide herself as a resting place for those whose bodies have never been recovered, the friends whose flesh has been mutilated beyond recognition. They are the dead who have become "too many to bury," who do not cease to exist and who seem to besiege surviving poets with pleas to witness on their behalf, to add their names to a litany and, in so doing, illuminate a senseless brutality.

These poems are testimonies to the value of a single human memory, political in the sense that there is no life apart from our common destiny. They are poems of passionate witness and confrontation. Responding to those who would state that politics has no place in poetry, that expressions of the human spirit in art should be isolated in aesthetics, she would add her voice to that of Neruda's: *we do not wish to please them.*

In her poems, we listen to the stark cry of the human spirit, stripped by necessity of its natural lyricism, deprived of the luxuries of cleverness and virtuosity enjoyed by poets of the north.

PREFACE

It is enough that the poet succeed in denying herself any justifiable indulgence.

In translating the work of contemporary Latin Americans, it is marginally possible to reproduce essential content, but in altering substance, there are always precipitates: those of music and atmosphere, specificities of tone. The unique characteristics are lost—in the case of Spanish, which has been called "the verbal medium of the spirit" (Castelar), its onomatopoeic and emphatic qualities, its syntactical freedom and a subtlety that survives abbreviation.

But in these we are not talking about the real difficulty—that of translating the human condition, the reality of one world, so that it may be intelligible to those of a world which has been spared its harshness.

Claribel Alegría's memory is suffused with death, the recurring vision of a young poet whose waterlogged body never washed ashore. She echoes the primitive wisdom: *there are lies more believable than the truth.* The cries of those who vanish assail her with accounts of torture and disappearance, the "blue theater" where a close friend witnessed the methodic dismemberment of a young man, whose flesh was sliced from him until his death. It is a world of live wires touched to genitals, of beatings, ice-water plunges, the parrot's perch, and of food, water, and sleep deprivation. The techniques of torture have been so refined that victims are forgiven their indiscretions. Few talk. The rest seem to have an almost yogic ability to sever mind from body. I was told of the "helmet," a sound chamber affixed to the skull that intensifies the screams of the victim until he can no longer bear the sound of his own voice.

That voice, after death, continues to cry out in the poetry of the impassioned. It becomes one of the "rosary of names" that must be whispered, both because they have become prayers and because their very mention can, at times, endanger the living.

PREFACE

Due to the social and familial circumstances of her life, Claribel
Alegría has not lived in her native El Salvador for many years.
Her residencies in Mexico, Chile, and Uruguay have broadened
her sense of geopolitical identity to embrace the continent. Her
years in North America and Europe have necessitated an integra-
tion of identities—a truce between a consciousness that is dis-
tinctly and essentially Latin American and one that is globally
aware of human fragility and mutual dependencies, social, polit-
ical, economic, and cultural—that has moved many Latin Ameri-
cans living abroad to question the validity of the term "exile" in
the modern world.

She is nostalgic for the music of her own language, for the fra-
ternity of dipping a warm tortilla into a common pot of beans and
meat. Her poetry fills with verdant jungles, volcanos, the glow of
their craters, the spillage of black rock; with olive trees twisted by
time, trees that are wisely neglected to assure that their fruit will
be moist and firm. We are immersed in memories of crumbling
aristocratic elegance: French wines, leather-spined books, English
roses that have since been supplanted for her by flowers splashing
down the volcanos in the arms of *campesino* children.

She carries within her the heavy, ancient blood of the Pipiles
and laces her language with a mestizo richness, words like the
stones of a land where mystery is still palpable. She is attentive to
her dreams, trusting them for news of her homeland, and she is
comfortable with the deceased, with the powers of amulets and
herbs and the gift of understanding the language of coincidence
and omen.

Had she realized her dream to become a painter, she would
have applied her pigments with a palette knife, with the decisive
strokes of a poet not afraid to speak plainly. Like Chagall, whom
she loves, her canvases would have reflected a private reality,
unique in its perceptions. In my days with her, I have grown to
understand that I have been in the presence of a woman whose

PREFACE

imagination was nurtured by a culture that persists to encourage wonder in the twentieth century, where the sixth sense is an empirical one.

In these poems, we have her account of her search for the grave of Garcia Lorca in Andalusia, undertaken while Franco was still alive. An impossible search. We are invited to explore the candle-lit village of Santa Ana where she spent her childhood, a place stripped of hope now, strafed by DDT and altered by the calm history of disintegration. We glimpse condors, tangos, the smoke of *copal*, a particular kind of light, *izote*, the constant presence of death, the face of an assassin transformed by traffic lights until he is seen as one of the many faces of his kind.

The poet is finally silenced herself, taking on the persona of the imprisoned, where she continues her poem "with tears, with fingernails and coal—the poem we are all writing."

It is now five years since Claribel Alegría and I met in Mallorca, and during this time more than 40,000 people have died in El Salvador at the hands of security forces. In our travels to bear witness to this brutal repression, we have more than once missed each other by days. She is at this writing at work in Managua. As a volume of poems is more likely to endure than any letter I might send, I would like to express my gratitude to Claribel for that summer of purpose and grace, for her dignity and dedication to justice. May we remain alive, continue to work, and meet again. Abrazos.

I wish to thank Maya Flakoll, onlie begetter of this work, for her impeccable faith and assistance, and the Alegría-Flakoll family for their hospitality and warmth during the summer of 1977 in Deya.

Carolyn Forché
1982

FLORES DEL VOLCÁN

FLOWERS FROM THE VOLCANO

HACIA LA EDAD JURASICA

Alguien los trajo a Palma
tenían el tamaño de una iguana
y comían insectos
y ratones.
El clima fue propicio
y empezaron a crecer
abandonaron las ratas
por los pollos
y seguían creciendo
se comían los perros
a más de un burro solitario
a los niños que andaban sueltos
por las calles.
Todas las cloacas
se atascaron
y huyeron al campo
se comieron las vacas
los corderos
y seguían creciendo
derrumbaron murallas
masticaban olivos
se rascaban el lomo
contra rocas salientes
y hubo derrumbes que bloquearon el camino
pero saltaron sobre los derrumbes
y están ahora en Valldemossa
y mataron al médico
del pueblo
y todos los vecinos
se asustaron
y corrieron despavoridos a esconderse.

2

honest expression of despising military

geological history

period of transition

TOWARD THE (JURASSIC) AGE

gire - river in France

Someone brought them to Palma
the size of an iguana
they ate insects and rats
the climate was favorable
they started to grow
they left rats for chickens and dogs
they ate more than one lonely donkey
children turned loose on the streets
the gutters were clogged as they
fled to the fields
they ate cows, sheep and kept growing
they tore down walls
they chewed up olive trees
they scratched their backs
on jutting rocks until
landslides blocked the roads
they leapt over the landslides
and now they are in Valldemossa
they killed the village doctor
and, frightened, the people hid
there are herbivores
and carnivores among them
the carnivores know one another
by the military caps that crown
their crests
but both are harmful
they devour plantations
and carry fleas the size of supper plates
they scratch against walls
until houses tumble
they are now in Valldemossa
and can only be killed

poem of strange being, being multiplied

develops w/ an unknown subject

beings damaged the environment can in an interrupted the people

beings are the military

not easy to get rid of them

expression of anti-military expression

3

against military in Central America

cry for peace

Hay herbívoros
y carnívoros se conocen
por las gorra castrense
que corona su cresta
pero ambos son dañinos
engullen plantaciones
y tienen pulgas del tamaño
de un gran plato
se rascan contra las paredes
y las casas se caen.
Están ahora en Valldemossa
y sólo pueden abatirse
por cohetes proyectados
desde aviones
pero nadie aguanta el hedor
cuando uno muere
y la gente protesta
y no hay manera
de enterrarlos.

by rockets dropped from planes
but no one can stand the stench
when one of them dies
the people protest that it is
impossible to bury them.

SANTA ANA A OSCURAS

A Maya

Hágase la oscurridad
decretó don Raimundo
y la luz se apagó
y quedó a oscuras Santa Ana.
Nunca fue muy brillante mi ciudad,
apenas bombillas de cuarenta vatios
aleteando contra algún interior,
iluminando un zurcido,
un planchado,
algún deber escolar.
Desde hace cien años
se apagaron las luces en Santa Ana.
Las mujeres ahora
ocupan velas para sus remiendos
y amanecen con ojos enrojecidos.
Los hombres se olvidaron de leer
y por las noches beben aguardiente
y salen a la calle
a disputar.
Sólo para los niños
es motivo de fiesta.
Nadie les exige que estudien sus lecciones.
Son tan pequeñas las letras
en los abecedarios
que es casi imposible discernirlas
y no aprenden su historia
de cuarenta vatios.
Todos los días
cuando se oculta el sol,
Mamá Clara, sentada en al andén
declama versículos de la Biblia.

SANTA ANA IN THE DARK

To Maya

Let there be darkness
declared Don Raimundo
the lights went out
Santa Ana grew dark
My village was never bright
only forty-watt bulbs
swaying in little shacks,
lighting up some mending
some ironing,
school lessons.
It has been one hundred years
since the death of light
in Santa Ana.
Now the women light
their work with candles
and wake red-eyed.
The men have forgotten books
and at night they drink
take to the streets, bicker.
Only the children have reason
to be glad.
No one forces them to study.
Their script letters shrink
until no one can see them.
They won't learn their forty-watt history.
Each day when the sun drops,
Mama Clara, sitting by the walk
recites Bible verses.

Los vecinos le piden
que les recite el génesis
y se maravillan
del poder de don Raimundo
que tuvo la osadía de apagar la luz.
Don Raimundo
tiene la costumbre de mandar.
Con un chasquear de dedos
pone
y dispone
y ejecuta
los problemas más espesos
del país.
El año pasado por ejemplo,
contaba el caporal,
le dije que faltaban más camiones
y en menos de una hora
había cinco
y hubo que llenarlos en seguida.
Por eso yo digo
que don Raimundo es listo
y Dios premia a los listos
y castiga a los que andamos tropezando.
La oscuridad se hizo
cuando murió mi padre.
Era el médico del pueblo
y trajo su linterna de Estelí.
El abuelo la trajo de París.
Nadie en Santa Ana
es capaz de producir su propia luz.
Cada vez que se apaga
una linterna
se opacan más las cosas

The neighbors ask her for Genesis
and they marvel at the power
of Don Raimundo
who had the gall to kill lights.
Don Raimundo is accustomed to command.
With the snap of his fingers
all is accomplished.
Last year alone,
said the foreman,
I told him we needed more trucks.
In less than an hour there were five.
We had to fill them like that.
That is why I tell you
Don Raimundo is clever.
God rewards the clever
while we go stumbling.
Darkness was created
when my father died.
He was the village doctor
who brought his lamp from Estelí.
His father before him
had carried it from Paris.
No one in Santa Ana
makes their own light.
Each time a lamp goes out
things grow murkier

y se mira sin ver
y se dice que sí con la cabeza
y no se entiende nada.
Ricardo encendia fósforos
para que nos viéramos las caras,
pero un día le cerraron el colegio.
José Ángel
tenía una linterna.
Se le había caído a alguien
y él la recogió.
Quería ser como mi padre
y lleva luz a casa de los otros,
pero murió de tétano.
Se derrumba nuestra casa
en Santa Ana
me escribió mi hermano
hace unos días.
Poco a poco
la fuimos abandonando
y los dejamos solo.
El jardín que antes se llenaba de pájaros
está vacío ahora.
El D.D.T. acabó con todos los pájaros
en Santa Ana
y las flores
no crecen como antes
en el jardín di mi casa.
Mi madre cuidaba los clavelones
y regaba el pasto
y le ayudaba al jazmín
a que subiera.
Ahora no está ella
y todo ha muerto

10

and you look without seeing
and say *yes* with your head
no one understands.
Ricardo lit matches
we could see our faces,
but the next day they closed down his school.
José Angel
had a lantern.
Someone dropped it
and he picked it up
wanting to be like my father
bringing his light to our homes.
He died of tetanus.
Our house in Santa Ana crumbles
writes my brother.
Little by little we abandon it,
one by one we leave it alone.
The garden once filled with birds is empty.
Poison finished Santa Ana's birds
and the flowers don't grow as before
in the garden of my house.
My mother tended the carnations,
she watered the grass
and nurtured the jasmin.
Now that she has gone
everything has died.

y los muertos se comen
a sus muertos
y se pudren las maderas
y se acabaron también
los zopilotes
y toda la podredumbre
se acumula.
Los rostros que en este álbum
me sonríen
oliendo a alcanfor
se han derrumbado ya:
Celia,
Isabel,
Margot.
Siguen engalanándose los domingos
para misa mayor
en Catedral.
Desde hace cuarenta años
es la misma rutina.
Se encuentran en el atrio
a la salida
y van al bar
(el que está frente al parque)
a tomar sorbetes de vainilla
y a transmitirse las noticias
y bendicen a Dios
porque son vírgenes
(todos los hombres son iguales
repiten siempre a coro)
y a las doce en punto
y se queda enterrada
entre flores de papel
y crucifijos.

The dead eat their dead.
The wood decomposes.
The vultures, because they have vanished,
rot piles upon rot.
The faces in this album
smile at me, smelling of camphor.
Celia,
Isabel,
Margot.
They still dress up on Sundays
for High Mass in the cathedral.
It has been this way forty years.
They meet in the vestry
as they go out
they walk to the cafe near the park
for vanilla sweets and to gossip
among themselves.
Thank God they are virgins!
(All men are alike)
At twelve each goes to her home
to be buried among
paper flowers and the silver Christ.

A veces en mis sueños
tropiezo con los ojos de don Santiago,
siempre los mismos ojos
que me esquivan,
el sombrero de paja
protegiendo del sol
su cabeza pelada,
el mismo monótono saludo,
los pies que diariamente
lo arrastran hacia el kiosco
y del kiosco a su casa
con un periódico en la mano.
Antes era brillante
don Santiago,
todo el pueblo lo afirma.
Tenía una farmacia
bien surtida
y vendía al crédito
y barato.
Pero un día se alzaron los campesinos
y él se declaró
contra la guardia nacional
y mandó don Raimundo
que le cerraran la farmacia
y murió su mujer
de paludismo
y sos hijos
huyeron
y no habla con nadie
desde entonces

Sometimes in my dreams
I stumble over the eyes
of Don Santiago,
always these eyes avoid mine.
A straw hat protects
his bald head from the sun.
The same dull hello.
The feet that daily drag him
toward the kiosk,
from the kiosk to his house
with his daily paper.
He was clever once.
The whole village knows it.
He had a pharmacy,
sold everything cheap or on credit.
One day the village rose up.
Santiago himself against the police.
Don Raimundo ordered his pharmacy closed
and his wife died of yellow fever.
His sons fled.
Since then he has spoken to no one.

y cada vez que en sueños
tropiezo con él
pienso que estoy
en el páramo de la muerte
y despierto temblando.
No importaba en la infancia.
Todo era verde entonces.
Crecíamos sin saber
que había luz en otras partes
y nos maravillábamos
cuando alguien
llevaba una linterna.
El sol
y la luna
nos bastaban;
el telón de luciérnagas
abriéndose y cerrándose
en la noche,
las nubes gordas
con bordes de plata,
el resplandor de Izalco,
los cocuyos,
las tormentas con truenos
y relámpagos
y Sirio
y Venus
y las siete cabritas
que brillan más
en el cielo de Santa Ana
y todo esto
es una manera de decir
que me asaltan a veces
unas ganas violentas
de volver.

Each time I stumble over him
in my dreams I think I am
in the open country of death
and I wake chilled.
It didn't matter
when we were young.
Everything was green.
We grew up without knowing
of light in other places
and we marveled when someone
carried a lamp.
Sun and moon were enough;
the curtain of fireflies opening,
closing in the night.
The fat clouds.
The glow of the crater Izalco.
The fireflies.
And the morning star, Sirius
and Seven Little Sisters
brighter in the darkness of Santa Ana
than anywhere else in the world.
All of this to tell you
I am desperate to go back.

SORROW

A Roque Dalton

I

Voces que vienen
que van
que se confunden
cuando sepas que he muerto
no pronuncies mi nombre
sombras amigas
que pregonan
que rompen un instante
la neblina
una mano sin dedos
tocando la guitarra
una sola vibración
desesperada
que se levanta
huye
sigo buscando a ciegas
me sostiene
se escapa
¿eres tú Victor Jara?
un enjambre de sombras
rostros que ya no existen
una palabra rota
pequeñas frases sueltas
que apenas si adivino:
listos para la muerte
listos para vencer
un eco que me llega
se deshace
verde que
y es ola
y estrella
y transparencia
puedo escribir los versos más tristes esta noche.

SORROW

To Roque Dalton

I

Voices that rise and are gone
cuando sepas que he muerto
no pronuncies mi nombre
(when you know that I have died
do not speak my name)
the dark shapes of friends
crying out
that break the fog an instant
a hand with no fingers
strumming a guitar
a single desperate sound
that lifts and escapes
I grope and it supports me
as it recedes.
Is that you, Victor Jara?
These shadows of faces
that no longer exist
a broken word
small phrases so scattered
I can barely catch them:
listos para la muerte
listos para vencer
(prepared for death
prepared to conquer death)
an echo reaches me, cut short
verde que
(green, I want you green)
It is a wave
a star
a transparency
puedo escribir los versos más tristes esta noche
(Tonight I can write the saddest verses)

19

II

Polvo asoleado
en el camino
no es difícil nombrar
los árboles
las calles
la torre de la iglesia
el río seco
pero hay una neblina enrarecida
que sólo cubre rostros
los rostros antes claros
se oscurecen
cuando quiero saber cómo llegar
a la tumba prohibida
del poeta
pregunto en al hotel
en al café
las miradas se turbian
las palabras
y los rostros se esfuman
y no entiendo
los ademanes vagos
las senales
el crimen fue en Granada
en su Granada
todo el mundo lo sabe
pero nadie es capaz
de un detalle preciso
de decir por ejemplo
allí mismo lo echaron
al borde de ese olivo
junto al cadáver joven
de un maestro con gafas

II

Sun drenches the road
it isn't difficult to name
the trees, the streets, the church tower
the dry riverbed but there is light fog
and it veils the faces that were clear
the faces once clear grow hazy
when I want to know how to reach
the hidden tomb of the poet
I ask at a hotel, in a cafe
the alarmed expressions, the words
and the faces vanish
I do not understand
vague gestures and directions
El crimen fue en Granada
en su Granada
(The crime was in Granada
in his Granada)
everyone knows that
but no one is capable
of the precise detail
of saying for example
they flung his body down
at the foot of that olive tree
beside the young body
of a schoolteacher in glasses

21

abro el mapa
me interno en el camino
polvoriento
rocoso
recojo algunas flores
y les sacudo el polvo
otro pueblo adelante
nadie sabe tampoco
sólo un viejo oficial
de arrugas amargadas
las mismas arrugas del camino
me responde arrogante
el poeta enemigo
barbotea
el maricón
y se aleja
encongiéndose de hombros
verde que te quiero verde
un polvo fino
obstinado
cubre los olivares
te negaron la lápida
ni siquiera un indicio
abro de nuevo el mapa
por aquí debe ser
doblé por la barranca
que se tragó los cuerpos
abajo el techo de la casa
el cuarto desolado
tu último peldaño
intangible
real
cien metros más allá
la Fuente Grande

I open the map
I set off down the dust-road
I pick some flowers
and shake the dust from them
another village ahead, another
no one knows here either
only an old official, his face
cracked with bitterness, the same
rutted grooves as in the road
he answers me arrogant
our enemy the poet
he mutters *that faggot*
he walks off
Verde que te quiero verde
(green I love you green)
a fine stubborn dust
covers the olive trees
there is no tombstone
there are no clues
I open the map again
it must be close
I skirt the ravine
the one that swallowed the bodies
below me the house roof
that desolate room, your last
stairstep, intangible, real
a hundred meters ahead, La Fuente Grande

no te pusieron lápida
te hicieron el honor
de arrancar los olivos
combatientes
torcidos
cuántos siglos de aceituna
los pies y las manos presos
sol a sol y luna a luna
pesan sobre vuestros huesos
sólo un árbol dejaron
un olivo
ni una piedra que diga
aquí yace el poeta
pero alguien dejó un árbol
un olivo
alguien que supo
lo dejó.

III

Un tatuaje en la frente
nos señala
un obstinado brillo
en la mirada
de animal en acecho
de vigilia
de llanto endurecido
nos olfateamos en el metro
nos buscamos los ojos
titubeantes
desviamos la mirada
y seguimos sin rumbo
por las calles heladas
nos apartamos del café

24

they didn't give you a grave marker
they did you the honor of tearing up
the twisted, the stubborn olive trees
cuántos siglos de aceituna
how many centuries of olives
los pies y las manos presos
the feet and the hands prisoners
sol a sol y luna a luna
sun to sun and moon to moon
pesan sobre vuestros huesos
weigh over your bones
they left only one tree, an olive
not even a stone reading
here lies the poet
but someone left a tree, an olive
someone knew and left it standing

III

This mark on our foreheads
betrays us, the obstinate gleam
in our eyes of hunted animals
of vigilance, of calloused tears
we sense one another in the Metro
we seek each other's glance then turn away
we walk aimlessly in cold streets
we avoid cafes

miramos de reojo
el periódico del quiosco
un olor a guayabo
nos asalta
la indiferencia del mundo
el mate atardecido
la burbuja punzante
del puchero
se ha dechecho la patria
se ha podrido
nos revolcamos en su podredumbre
y la gente se aparta
y no sabemos si es nuestro sudor
o la carroña de la patria
un vaho pegajoso
nos envuelve
un vaho con tufo a desamparo
a sueños estancados
a no tener un cinco en el bolsillo
nos obliga a encorvarnos
bajo el cuello grasiento del abrigo
seguimos nuestra marcha
husmeando al compañero
al mundo nada le importa
yira, yira
nos conocemos por la mueca
por la mirada húmeda
caminamos sin prisa
a la deriva
en busca de algún sitio
donde poder lavarnos
el tufo
la vergüenza

we smell *guayabo*
the indifference of the world
the evening maté
the quick smell of bubbling stew
our country has fallen apart
it has gone bad
we roll in its filth
people avoid us
we don't know if it is our sweat
or the rotten taint of our land
a foul breath surrounds us
fumes that stink of helplessness
of stagnant dreams
of not having even small change
it forces us to tuck our heads
under the greasy collars of our coats
and keep walking, searching out comrades
al mundo nada le importa
yira, yira
(nothing matters to the world
yira, yira)
we know one another by our grimace
by our damp eyes
we walk unhurried
we drift in search of a place
where we can wash ourselves
of the offensive odor of shame

y huimos a los baños
donde todos los exiliados se congregan
y nadie tiene un cinco
y los hongos pululan
se nos llenan de hongos
los dedos de los pies
pero no importa
hay que arrancarse el tufo
de exiliado
de perro callejero
preferibles los hongos
que nos pican
nos desangran los pies
nos gritan desde adentro
me moriré en París con aguacero
un día del cual tengo ya el recuerdo.

IV

Obstinadas
confusas
me llegan las noticias
hechos truncados
fríos
frases contradictorias
que me acosan
así llegó tu muerte
Roque Dalton
la implacable noticia
de tu muerte
en los signos borrosos
de un periódico
en las exangües voces
de la radio

we flee to the public baths
where all exiles congregate
and no one has even small change
the fungi pullulate
the cracks between our toes swell with fungi
but that does not matter
we must scrub off the stench of exile
we are stray dogs
it is better to have itching fungi
leaving our feet bloody
leaving a shriek within us
me moriré en París con aguacero
un día del cual tengo ya el recuerdo
(I will die in Paris with a heavy rain shower
on a day of which I still have memory)

IV

Stubborn
confused
the news comes to me
truncated facts
cold, contradictory sentences
that pursue me
that is how your death arrived, Roque Dalton
the implacable news of your death
in the smudged headlines
your death in the bloodless voice of the radio

en imágenes rotas
imprecisas.
Fuiste atalaya
lumbre
con orgullo de sable
cortaste la tiniebla
y envolvieron tu muerte
en la neblina
es peligroso Roque
ir pregonando al Che
a Jesús
a Sandino
ignorar al caudillo
abrir los ojos
sentir que tu memoria
desencadena llagas
y cada llaga es llama
que se levanta y vuela
siguen llegando ecos
acusaciones falsas
y nunca sabré quién te mató
pero estás muerto
Roque Dalton
y envolvieron tu muerte
en la neblina.

V

Huimos a los museos
son casi tan baratos
como los baños públicos
vagamos por las salas
nos hundimos por horas
en un sofá de cuero

it arrived without precision
in broken images
you were a lookout
a beacon slicing through fog
it is dangerous, Roque
to go about proclaiming Che
Jesus and Sandino
to ignore the real boss
to open your eyes
to feel that your own memory
opens wounds, each wound
a small flame rising
the echoes are still coming back
the false accusations
I'll never know who killed you
but you are dead, Roque Dalton,
and they wrap your death in fog.

V

We flee to the museums
they are nearly as cheap as public baths
we wander through salons
we sink into leather sofas

pretendiendo estudiar
un Corot
un Cézanne
y si el guardia se acerca
proferimos palabras
entusiasmos
y sequimos sentados otro rato
cierro los ojos
y surgen los olivos
los esclavos
cobran relieve la noche
el alba
el día
el mediodía
me refugio en los brazos
de la madre cultura
y descanso mis pies
llenos de hongos
los museos
los templos
otra vez surgen los esclavos
queriéndose evadir
de sus cadenas
de su matriz de piedra
que los fija
me esfuerzo en recordar
a la Pietá
al cristo con un pie
al cristo infante
los esclavos resurgen
los olivos
sus cuerpos retorcidos
me persiguen

and sit for hours pretending to study
a Corot, a Cézanne
if the guard comes near us
we exchange enthusiasms
and stay longer
I close my eyes
the olive trees loom over me
the slaves
I see the outlines of night
dawn, day and midday
I take refuge in the arms of Mother Culture
and rest my infested feet in museums
again the slaves loom before me
trying to escape the stones that imprison them
I force myself to remember the Pietà
the Christ with one foot
the infant Christ
the slaves loom up
the olives
their twisted torsos haunt me

salgo a la calle
a caminar sin rumbo
su mirada sin ojos
su deseo truncado
andaluces de Jaén
aceituneros altivos
decidme en el alma ¿quién
quién levantó los olivos?

VI

Sólo mis pasos
en la acera
de una taverna oscura
llegan ecos de tango
de milonga
olor a vino agrio
y a tabaco
me apresuro a la esquina
a la luz de neon que parpadea
una voz me detiene
una pregunta
el rostro se ilumina
y es azul
se vuelve rojo
grana
mientras busco en mi bolso la cerilla
una máscara blanca
que me observa
y se vuelve morada
es tu verdugo
Roque
lo ilumino de cerca

I return to the street to wander
their eyeless faces
their maimed desires
andaluces de Jaén
(Andalucians of Jaén)
aceituneros altivos
(haughty olive workers)
decidme en al alma ¿quién
(tell me in spirit who)
quién levantó los olivos?
(who raised up the olives?)

VI

Only my footsteps on the walk
from a dark tavern
echoes of tangos, milongas
odors of sour wine and smoke
I hurry to the corner
the blinking neon
a voice detains me
a question
a face lights up
and is blue
it turns red
scarlet
I search for matches in my bag
a white mask
it observes me
it turns violet
it is your assassin, Roque
I light the face

35

y sólo es un muchacho
aún imberbe
que con facciones laxas
me sonríe
la luz de nuevo azul
y ya se aleja
es tu verdugo
es él
y no me atrevo
y lo dejo pasar
y me averguenzo.

VII

¿Quien sembró los barrotes?
sólo una luz palúdica
me llega desde afuera
no hay sol
no hay pájaros
no hay verdes
en trozos verticales
me han recortado el cielo
toco mi piel tirante
a los lejos escucho mi jadeo
necesito ser yo
salir de esta neblina
sacudirme el terror.
Con un carbón pulido
escribo algunas letras:
mi soledad
mi . . .
comienzan las voces
a llegarme
el telón de fondo

it is only a boy still beardless
he smiles at me
the light is blue again
he moves off
it is your assassin
it is he
I don't dare
I let him pass
I am ashamed

VII

Who raised the bars?
a gray light filters from outside
there is no sun
there are no birds, no foliage
they have sliced away the sky
I touch my stiff skin
I listen to my own panting
as from a distance
I need to remain myself
to leave the fog
throw off the terror
with a chip of coal I begin to write:
my loneliness, my—
the voices begin coming toward me
this backdrop of cries

de las voces
punteado por un grito.
Un súbito silencio
de pavor
y otra vez con más brío.
A callar
nos chilla el carcelero
haciendo sonar llaves
en las rejas
nadie lo escucha
las voces de todos
confundidas
en un solemne
y obstinado coro
que sube
crece
se desborda.
Desde mi soledad
acompañada
alzo la voz
pregunto
y la respuesta es clara:
soy Georgina
soy Nelson
soy Raúl
de neuvo el torturado
su aullido
el silencio
con los ojos abiertos
me recuesto en el catre
ni una raja de luz
se apagó el aullido
empiezo a contar nombres
mi rosario de nombres

punctuated by a scream
a sudden, a terrified silence
they start up again more loudly
shut up! the turnkey shouts
clanking his keys on the bars
no one listens to it
the voices of all
mingling in a solemn
a stubborn chorus that rises
swells, overflows
from my solitude I raise my voice
I ask and the answer is clear:
I am Georgina
I am Nelson
I am Raúl
again the tortured one
his howl and silence
I stretch out on my cot
with my eyes open
and not so much as a fissure of light
the screams are cut
I begin counting the names
my rosary of names

pienso en el otro
el próximo
que dormirá en mi catre
y escuchará el ruido
de los goznes
y cagará aquí mismo
en ese cano
llevando a cuestas
su cuota de terror
vuelvo obstinada
a mi rosario
no estoy sola
están ellos
los huéspedes de paso
apenas nos separa
una hoja de tiempo
una delgada tela
que desgarro
y hay vino
y guitarras
y hay tabaco
están Víctor
Violeta
el poeta pastor
salto alegre del catre
y tropiezo con Roque
llevo un dedo a mis labios
y se callan las risas
las guitarras
un enjambre de ojos
me acompaña
mientras grabo en el muro:
"más solos están ellos
que nosotros."

40

I think about the other
the next one who will sleep here
on my cot and listen
to the groaning hinges
and shit right here in this open pipe
hunched beneath his quota of terror
I return to my rosary
I am not alone
they are here
the transient guests
only a tissue of time
a tissue separates us
there is wine
there are guitars, tobacco
there are Victor and Violeta
the shepherd poet
I leap from my cot
and stumble into Roque
I raise my finger to my lips
the laughter dies, the guitars, the eyes
I scratch on the wall:
they are more alone than we are.

Y la octava

De nuevo el aullido
¿brota de mi
de ti?
Inexorable
grave
Melpómene
me escruta.
Paso frente a sus ojos
desde el centra turquesa
del mosaico
su fulgor me persigue
existen los barrotes
nos rodean
también existe el catre
y sus angulos duros
y el poema río
que nos sostiene a todos
y es tan substantivo
como el catre
el poema que todos escribimos
con lágrimas
y uñas
y carbón.
Se terminó la fiesta
hay colillas deshechas en el suelo
están rotos los vasos
y nos quedamos solos
sin guitarras
sin voz para cantar
y surge la pregunta
el desafío
decidme en el alma ¿quién
quién levantó los barrotes?

And the eighth

Again, the scream
is it mine, is it coming from me?
From you, is it yours?
Gravely Melpomene studies me
I pass before her eyes
from the turquoise heart of a mosaic
her resplendence follows me
the bars do exist
they surround us
the cot also exists
with its hard sides
the river poem
that sustains us all
and is as substantial as the cot
the poem we are all writing
with tears, with fingernails and coal
the fiesta is over
the cigarette butts on the floor
the glasses are in shards
and we remain alone without guitars
without voices to sing
and the question rises, the challenge
tell me, in spirit, who
who raised up this prison's bars?

FLORES DEL VOLCÁN

A Roberto y Ana María

Catorce volcanes se levantan
en mi país memoria
en mi país de mito
que día a día invento
catorce volcanes de follaje y piedra
donde nubes extrañas se detienen
y a veces el chillido
de un pájaro extraviado.
¿Quién dijo que era verde mi país?
es más rojo
es más gris
es más violento:
el Izalco que ruge
exigiendo más vidas
los eternos chacmol
que recogen la sangre
y los que beben sangre
del chacmol
y los huérfanos grises
y el volcán babeando
toda esa lava incandescente
y el guerrillero muerto
y los mil rostros traicionados
y los niños que miran
para contar la historia.
No nos quedó ni un reino
uno a uno cayeron
a lo largo de América
el acero sonaba
en los palacios
en las calles
en los bosques

FLOWERS FROM THE VOLCANO

To Roberto and Ana Maria

[handwritten: Nation Emblem]

Fourteen volcanos rise *[handwritten: → El Salvador]*
in my remembered country
in my mythical country.
Fourteen volcanos of foliage and stone
where strange clouds hold back
the screech of a homeless bird. *[handwritten: color for hope and peace]*
Who said that my country was green?
It is more red, more gray, more violent: *[handwritten: not place of peace]*
Izalco roars, *[handwritten: blood pain]*
taking more lives.
Eternal Chacmol collects blood, *[handwritten: → military heads]*
the gray orphans
the volcano spitting bright lava *[handwritten: Unity of violent]*
and the dead *guerrillero* *[handwritten: nature and politics]*
and the thousand betrayed faces,
the children who are watching
so they can tell of it. *[handwritten: violence is natural]*
Not one kingdom was left us. *[handwritten: habitant → live]*
One by one they fell *[handwritten: among volcanos]*
through all the Americas.
Steel rang in palaces,
in the streets,
in the forests *[handwritten: lost cities > can't preserve]*

[handwritten: Tlaloc - god of justice]

45

y saqueaban el templo
los centauros
y se alejaba el oro
y se sigue alejando
en barcos yanquis
el oro del café
mezclado con la sangre
mezclado con el látigo
y la sangre.
El sacerdote huía
dando gritos
en medio de la noche
convocaba a sus fieles
y abrían el pecho de un guerrero
para ofrecerle al Chac
su corazón humeante.
Nadie cree en Izalco
que Tlaloc esté muerto
por más televisores
heladeras
toyotas
el ciclo ya se acerca
es extraño el silencio del volcán
desde que dejó de respirar
Centroamérica tiembla
se derrumbó Managua
se hundió la tierra en Guatemala
el huracán Fifi
arrasó con Honduras
dicen que los yanquis lo desviaron
que iba hacia Florida
y lo desviaron

and the (centaurs sacked the temple)
Gold disappeared and continues
to disappear on *yanqui* ships,
the (golden coffee mixed) with blood.
The priest flees screaming
in the middle of the night
he calls his followers
and they open the *guerrilleros* chest
so as to offer the Chac
his smoking heart.
No one believes in Izalco
that Tlaloc is dead
despite television,
refrigerators,
Toyotas.
The cycle is closing,
strange the volcano's silence
since it last drew breath.
Central America trembled,
Managua collapsed.
In Guatemala the earth sank
Hurricane Fifi flattened Honduras.
They say the *yanquis* turned it away,
that is was moving toward Florida
and they forced it back.

[handwritten margin annotations:]
...ing of being ruled by eternal powers
gold Spaniards
allusion to outsiders Spaniards brought those to new world
yankee
this situation should end can't live in such violence, poverty must end
eruption of volcano was the will of god to end something

el oro del café
desembarca en New York
allí los tuestan
lo trituran
lo envasan
y le ponen un precio.
"Siete de junio
noche fatal
bailando el tango
la capital."
Desde la terraza ensombrecida
se domina el volcán San Salvador
le suben por los flancos
mansiones de dos pisos
protegidas por muros
de cuatro metros de alto
le suben rejas y jardines
con rosas de Inglaterra
y araucarias enanas
y pinos de Uruguay
un poco más arriba
ya en el cráter
hundidos en el cráter
viven gentes del pueblo
que cultivan sus flores
y envían a sus niños a venderlas.
El ciclo ya se acerca
las flores cuscatlecas
se llevan bien con la ceniza
crecen grandes y fuertes
y lustrosas

The golden coffee is unloaded
in New York where
they roast it, grind it
can it and give it a price.
Siete de Junio
noche fatal
bailando el tango
la capital.
From the shadowed terraces
San Salvador's volcano rises.
Two-story mansions
protected by walls
four meters high
march up its flanks
each with railings and gardens,
roses from England
and dwarf *araucarias,*
Uruguayan pines.
Farther up, in the crater
within the crater's walls
live peasant families
who cultivate flowers
their children can sell.
The cycle is closing,
Cuscatlecan flowers
thrive in volcanic ash,
they grow strong, tall, brilliant.

bajan los niños del volcán
bajan como la lava
con sus ramos de flores
como raíces bajan
como ríos
se va acercando el ciclo
los que viven en casas de dos pisos
protegidas del robo por los muros
se asoman al balcón
ven esa ola roja
que desciende
y ahogan en whisky su temor
sólo son probres niños
con flores del volcán
con jacintos
y pascuas
y mulatas
pero crece la ola
que se los va a tragar
porque el chacmol de turno
sigue exigiendo sangre
porque se acerca el ciclo
porque Tlaloc no ha muerto.

The volcano's children
flow down like lava
with their bouquets of flowers,
like roots they meander
like rivers the cycle is closing.
The owners of two-story houses
protected from thieves by walls
peer from their balconies
and they see the red waves descending
and they drown their fears in whiskey.
They are only children in rags
with flowers from the volcano,
with *Jacintos* and *Pascuas* and *Mulatas*
but the wave is swelling,
today's Chacmol still wants blood,
the cycle is closing,
Tlaloc is not dead.

inspiration → image from children
coming down from
volcano / lava

about nationally identity
past - volcano rituals, culture
now - injustice pol. econ

ERAMOS TRES

A Paco, a Rodolfo

Era invierno con nieve
era de noche
hoy es día de verdes
de pájaros
de sol
día de cenizas
y lamentos
me empuja el viento
me lleva por el puente
por la tierra agrietada
por el arroyo seco
rebosante de plásticos y latas
la muerte cobra vida
aquí en Deyá
los arroyos
los puentes
mis muertos acechando
en cada esquina
las rejas inocentes
de un balcón
el reflejo borroso
de mis muertos
me sonríen de lejos
se despiden
salen del cemeterio
forman muro
se me vuelve translúcida
la piel
me tocan a la puerta
gesticulan
era de piedra el puente
era de noche
los brazos enlazados
por el vaivén de un canto

WE WERE THREE

To Paco and Rodolfo

It was winter,
there was snow,
it was night,
this is a green day
of doves and sun
of ashes and cries.
The wind pushes me
across the bridge
over the cracked earth
through a dry streambed
strewn with cans.
Death comes to life
here in Deya,
the *torrente*
the stone bridge.
My dead wait
at every corner,
the innocent grillwork of balconies
the filmed mirror of my dead.
They smile from the distance
and wave to me,
they leave the cemetery,
a wall of the dead.
My flesh emits light
and they come to my door
waving their arms.
The bridge was stone,
it was night,
our arms circled each other,
we swayed to our songs,

como pequeñas nubes congeladas
nos salía el aliento
de las bocas
era invierno con nieve
eramos tres
hoy la tierra está seca
reverbera
se me caen los brazos
estoy sola
montan guardia mis muertos
me hacen señas
me asaltan por la radio
en el periódico
el muro de mis muertos
se levanta
se extiende de Aconcagua
hasta el Izalco
continúan su lucha
marcan rumbos
era de piedra el puente
era de noche
nadie sabe decir
cómo murieron
sus voces perseguidas
se confunden
murieron en la cárcel
torturados
se levantan mis muertos
tienen rabia
las calles están solas
me hacen guiños
soy cementerio apátrida
no caben.

our breath rose from our mouths
in small, crystalline clouds,
it was winter,
there was snow,
we were three.
Today the earth is dry
and resounds like a drum,
my arms fall to my sides,
I am alone.
My dead stand watch
and send signals to me,
they assail me
in the radio and paper.
The wall of my dead
rises and reaches from Aconcagua to Izalco.
The bridge was stone,
it was night,
no one can say
how they died.
Their persecuted voices are one voice
dying by torture in prison.
My dead arise, they rage.
The streets are empty
but my dead wink at me.
I am a cemetery,
I have no country
and they are too many to bury.

SE HACE TARDE DOCTOR

Llegó hasta El Salvador sobre una mula.
Venía de Estelí,
de Nicaragua,
de aquella tierra azul
con olor a becerros
y a tiste.
Estudió bajo la luz de los faroles.
Ganó medalla de oro.
Pero no.
Quiero ser más precisa.
Lo veo.
llevándonos a cuestas por el patio,
haciendo de león para asustarnos,
mirándome a los ojos y diciendo:
"para un viejo
una niña
siempre tiene el pecho de cristal".
Recuerdo:
mi sofocante asombro,
mis preguntas,
las paredes de cal,
mis pantorillas
que nunca me engordaban,
los arcos,
el jazmín,
el porte de mi madre,
su manojo de llaves
en el cinto.
A veces, por la noche,
mientras la luna
alumbraba los gatos de las tejas
y se oía chirriar a las cigarras,

IT'S GROWING LATE, DOCTOR

He came from El Salvador on a mule,
he came from Estelí,
from Nicaragua,
from that blue country
with the smell of calves and *tiste*.
He studied under streetlamps,
he won a gold medal.
But no.
I want to be more exact.
I see him carrying us on his back on the patio
playing the lion to frighten us,
looking into my eyes saying:
for an old man
a child always
has a heart of glass.
I remember my choked wonder, my questions.
The whitewashed walls,
my thin legs that never rounded,
the arches, jasmin, my mother's carriage.
The ring of keys at her belt.
Sometimes at night
while the moon
lit the cats on the roof
and crickets shrilled

nos habló de Sandino,
de sus hombres,
de las largas marchas por la selva,
de los marinos yanquis,
desde arriba silbando sus helldivers
para herir la columna.
Nos hablaba también de la cesárea,
de descubrir al niño acurrucado.
En días de neblina
subimos al volcán,
el rocío lamiéndome las piernas,
con orquídeas las ramas
y con musgo.
Subíamos al sol,
hasta la cumbre,
otra vez hasta el sol de Centroamérica.
Yo quería correr,
era el ama de casa;
salir a buscar nidos,
alisaba el mantel.
Mi hermano, canturreando,
hacía saltar piedras
sobre el lago de azufre,
de esmeralda.
Tu aire de patriarca
nos cohibía.
Presidías la mesa
como un señor feudal.
Quiero hablarte de mí,
de cómo soy.
Conservo mi egoísmo,
sigo haciendo complots
para ganar cariño.

he told us of Sandino
of his men
of long marches through jungle
of the *yanqui* Marines
whistling their helldivers
down the column.
He told us of cesareans,
of discovering the crouched child.
On foggy days we climbed
the volcano,
mist licking our legs,
the branches with orchids and moss.
We climbed to the sun,
the very peak
once more to the sun of Central America.
I wanted to run,
I was the mother to look after a nest of birds.
I smoothed our tablecloth.
My brother, chanting
skipped stones over the sulphur lake.
Your patriarchal air
frightened us.
You ruled the table
like a feudal lord.
I want to tell you
about me, how I am.
I am still selfish.
I continue weaving
plots to win love.

Se hace tarde, doctor.
Los dos amanecimos
junto a un niño enfermo,
nos aburrimos
entre gentes extrañas,
hicimos el ridículo,
tropezamos,
caímos,
tuvimos que aceptar.
Me legaste riquezas:
Sandino, por ejemplo,
la unión de Centroamérica,
el afán de tener una cesárea.
El exilio nos duele.
Nos incomoda a veces
nuestro papel de padres.
Sigo pensando en mí con prioridad.
No soy tu hija ahora,
so tu cómplice,
tu socio.
Mis derrotas,
mis luchas,
me han hecho el llanto fácil.
Pienso en ti mientras digo.
Pienso en mí,
en las cosas que ocurren.

It's growing late, Doctor.
We have both stayed
until dawn beside a sick child,
we grew bored among strangers,
we were ridiculous,
we stumbled and fell,
we had to accept that.
You left me riches:
Sandino, for example,
the Union of Central America,
the need to have a cesarean.
Exile destroys us.
At times, being parents annoys us.
I still think of myself first.
I am not your daughter now,
but your accomplice, your partner.
My defeats, my struggles
have made the tears easy.
I think of you while I think of myself,
of things that happen.

CARTA AL TIEMPO

Estimado señor:
Esta carta la escribo en mi cumpleaños.
Recibí su regalo. No me gusta.
Siempre y siempre lo mismo.
Cuando niña, impaciente lo esperaba;
me vestía de fiesta
y salía a la calle a pregonarlo.
No sea usted tenaz.
Todavía lo veo
jugando al ajedrez con el abuelo.
Al principio eran sueltas sus visitas;
se volvieron muy pronto cotidianas
y la voz del abuelo
fue perdiendo su brillo.
Y usted insistía
y no respetaba la humildad
de su carácter dulce
y sus zapatos.
Después me cortejaba.
Era yo adolescente
y usted con ese rostro que no cambia.
Amigo de mi padre
para ganarme a mí.
Pobrecito del abuelo.
En su lecho de muerte
estaba usted presente,
esperando el final.
Un aire insospechado
flotaba entre los muebles.
Parecían más blancas las paredes.
Y había alguien más,
usted le hacía señas.
Él le cerró los ojos al abuelo
y se detuvo un rato a contemplarme.

LETTER TO TIME

Dear Sir:
I write this letter on my birthday.
I received your gift. I don't like it.
It is always the same.
As a girl I waited impatient.
I dressed up and went to the street
to talk about it.
Don't be stubborn.
I can still see you playing
chess with my grandfather.
At first your visits were rare.
Soon they became daily
and grandfather's voice
lost its luster.
And you insisted
without respect for his humility,
his gentle soul, his shoes.
Later you courted me.
I was still young
and you with your unchanging face.
A friend of my father's
with one eye on me.
Poor grandfather.
You waited at his death bed for the end.
The walls paled
and there was something else.
An unknown air
floated among the things in the room.
You called to him
and he closed my grandfather's eyes
and looked at me.

Le prohibo que vuelva.
Cada vez que lo veo
me recorre las vértebras el frío.
No me persiga más,
se lo suplico.
Hace años que amo a otro
y ya no me interesan sus ofrendas.
¿Por qué me espera siempre en las vitrinas,
en la boca del sueño,
bajo el cielo indeciso del domingo?
Sabe a cuarto cerrado su saludo.
Lo he visto el otro día con los niños.
Reconocí su traje:
el mismo tweed de entonces
cuando era yo estudiante
y usted amigo de mi padre.
Su ridículo traje de entretiempo.
No vuelva,
le repito.
No se detenga más en mi jardín.
Se asustarán los niños
y las hojas se caen:
las he visto.
¿De qué sirve todo esto?
Se va a reír un rato
con esa risa eterna
y seguirá saliéndome al encuentro.
Los niños,
mi rostro,
las hojas,
todo extraviado en sus pupilas.
Ganará sin remedio.
Al comenzar mi carta lo sabía.

I forbid you to come back.
Each time I see you my spine stiffens.
Stop following me.
I beg you.
It has been years since I loved another
and your gifts are no longer of interest.
Why do you wait for me in shop windows,
in sleep's mouth,
beneath the uncertain Sunday sky?
Your greeting tastes of musty rooms.
I saw you the other day with the children.
I knew your suit, the same tweed
when you were my father's friend
and I was a student.
Your ridiculous autumn suit.
Do not come back.
I insist.
Do not linger in my garden.
The children will frighten
and the leaves drop.
I have seen them.
What is the use of all of this?
You will laugh a while
and with that unending laugh
you will still turn up.
The children,
my face,
leaves,
all nothing in your eyes.
You will win.
I knew it when I began.

SOY RAIZ

Oh vida por vivir y ya vivida
tiempo que vuelve en una marejada
y se retira sin volver el rostro
—Octavio Paz, *Piedra de Sol*

Más que piedra pulida
más que mañana ocaso
más que sueño de arbol
y de flor
y de fruto
soy raíz
un avanzar reptado
de raíz
sin fulgor
sin futuro
ciego de prefecías
endureciendo el suelo
en el que ondeo
saboreando el maná
de la desdicha
de la opacidad
del pájaro sin alas
del alba sin centella
de la nube sin brillo
de las horas que pasan
sin presagios
ondeando
serpeando
la raíz
quizá desenterrando
el relámpago aquel
la piedra aquella
que una vez en la playa
reptando entre malezas
a solas

I AM ROOT

More than polished stone
more than morning dusk
more than the dream of the tree
and those of flower and fruit
I am root
a winding, crawling root
without luster, without a future
blind to any vision
hardening the ground
as I work through it
testing the fallen bread
of misfortune
the opacity of wingless birds
the overshadowed dawn
and its leaden clouds
hours that pass without dark messages
an undulating, twining root
perhaps bringing up from the ground
that lightning, that stone
once on the beach moving among
weeds, alone among rubbish, searching

sobre escombros
avanzando
buscando
dividiéndose
en vértigos-segmentos
conicienta raíz
mortal raíz
buceadora en mi zona de tinieblas
caligrafía oscura
heredad de patíbulo
y de cábala
venenosa raíz
envuelta por el tiempo
de un espacio
espejo de mí misma
sin humedad
sin agua
tu cuerpo sabe a tierra
tu corteza a verano
encarcelado
y no buscas resquicio
buscas muerte
una muerte tranquila
enmascarada
di días sin presagios
y de tiempo
sin fechas
de rostros que son grises
y apacibles
y de horas
sin pájaros
en que simplemente
se deshace el instante.

cinereous root, mortal root
diver of my darkest regions
obscure calligraphy
inheritance of gallows, of cabala
poison root, imprisoned
by the time of a place
mirror of myself without water, thirsty
your blood tastes of the earth
your bark, summer
imprisoned, you don't look
for openings, you look for death
a quiet death, disguised
as days without omens
and as time without dates
and the gray willing faces of the hours
without birds where an instant
simply dissolves

Mi vida por venir
no me consume
en mis labios hay grietas
y mi rostro es de piedra
y le cierro el paso
a la tormenta
y sigilosamente me sumerjo
en el eterno mar
que ya no avanza
y se acaba el rumor
y el torbellino
y las apariciones
y desapariciones
y todos los sueños
en que simplemente
nos soñamos
y los residuos
de un amor espada
y de aquel otro amor
a escondidas
y los nombres de Eros
y de Tánatos
todo se desvanece
tu canto de cristal
no llega nunca
mi tu caricia de agua
ni tus labios
ni los dientes filosos
de tu amor

the life I've yet to live
does not inspire me
in my lips there are crevices
and my face is stone
I do not allow a storm to enter
silently, I submerge myself
in a sea which no longer moves
the murmur ends
the appearances and disappearances
all dreams in which we can only
dream of ourselves
the remains of that daggered love
and the other, hidden love
the names of Eros and Thanatos
everything vanishes
your crystal song never reaches me
nor your wet touch, nor your lips
nor the teeth of your love

recojo mis fragmentos
y voy reptando
a ciegas
voy olfateando el mar
en el que un día
el olvido me cubra
la memoria
y no sienta punzadas
ni reclamos
ni miedo
y sólo sea ún giro
un remolino
en la tumba de ague
que me cubra.

I gather my fragments and slip away,
I slither, I smell the sea
in which one day my memory will be
buried and I will not know pain
demands, or fear
and I will be then no more
than a calm spin in a tomb of water.

MIS ADIOSES

El jet de la tarde me arranca de Ezeiza.
Me lanza contra la pared
de la cordillera
impregnada de sombras.
Me arranca de los adioses,
de la última vez
entre rostros rioplatenses,
de la noche en el acuario verdeazul
con humo flotando como plankton
y monstruos marinos
se deslizan por la luz
al compás de un tango.
Desde mi ventana,
la mancha morada de las pampas.
Repito a solas mis adioses,
los prenso
entre las hojas de un libro
que no leo.
El horizonte se encoge
y nos asalta.
Nos pasa el Aconcagua
con su joroba rosa.
Santiago deslumbra en el crepúsculo.
Casi sin verlo
recorro el aeropuerto,
casi sin recordar las otras veces,
los otros adioses
que he dicho aquí,
esquivando esta despedida
solitaria,
definitiva.

MY GOOD-BYES

The afternoon jet plucks me from Ezeiza.
It hurls me against the shadowy
wall of the *cordillera.*
It plucks me from my good-byes,
from my final moment
among the faces of the Rio de la Plata,
from that night in the blue aquariums
where smoke drifted like plankton clouds
and we were sea-life sliding
through the night to the beat of a tango.
From my window,
a violet glimpse of the pampas.
I repeat my good-byes in silence,
pressing them in a book
I will never read.
The horizon gathers itself
and comes toward us.
The rosy humpback of Aconcagu
lumbers past,
Santiago sparkles in the dust.
I pace the airport terminal
without looking at it,
almost without recalling
other times, other good-byes
avoiding this last one,
so final and definite.

Lejos de mi ventana
una luna nueva
se hunde en el Pacifico.
Pienso en los años,
los amigos,
la geografía.
América es grande,
me digo.
Un bloque de piedra
torturado.
Su yerba,
sus árboles,
sus voces crecen,
trepan,
entierran nichos de piedra estéril.
América es una viva piedra verde.
Es difícil América,
es oscura,
es verde,
es difícil.
La estrangula la selva.
El sol
le siembra desiertos.
Sus hombres se pierden
entre arrugas
y ríos.
Escazú,
Mombo,
Momotombo,
Chingo,
Izalco:
su pregunta brumosa
me persigue.

From my window
a fresh moon
sinks to the Pacific.
I think of years, friends, geography.
America is vast, I tell myself.
A slab of pained stone.
Its grasses, its trees, its voices
grow, spread, overrun
niches of sterile rock.
America is a green, a living stone.
America is difficult.
It is somber, green, difficult.
The jungle has it by the throat.
The sun seeds its deserts.
Its people are lost
between furrows and rivers.
Escazu
Mombo
Momotombo
Chingo
Izalco:
a smoking question pursues me.

Santa Ana.
Mi gente una vez más.
El patio con verdes
y con sombras,
la ceremonia del refresco,
el chaparrón,
la interminable fila de visitas,
los lentos murmullos
de la tarde,
el monólogo de la tía Virginia,
de su amor perdido
y de sus gatos.
Cementerio de razas
es mi valle:
cementerio de nombres—
Sihuatehuacán,
valle de las mujeres hermosas—
de tribus anónimas,
lampiñas,
de conquistadores con barba
y caballo,
de doncellas inmoladas
ante la mirada jade
del jaguar.
Mi América es sangre derramada:
una puesta en escena de Caín y Abel,
una lucha sin tregua
con el hambre,
la rabia,
la impotencia.
Me arranco,
me voy.
Apenas me importa un sollozo.

78

Santa Ana.
My people once again.
The terrace with its foliage of shadows,
the ceremony of trembling pitchers,
sudden rains,
the endless string of visitors
and the slow whispers of an afternoon,
Aunt Virginia's monologue
of her lost love and her cats.
My valley is a burial ground of races,
a cemetery of names—
Sihuatehuacán,
a valley of beautiful women
and smooth-skinned tribes,
bearded *conquistadores*
horses
and virgins sacrificed beneath
the jade gaze of the jaguar.
My America is spilled blood,
the theater of Cain and Abel,
a struggle with no quarter given
against starvation, rage or impotence.
But I am leaving.
It cannot be worth this.

Como un bocadillo
me trago a Guatemala,
sin saborearla,
sin la grave presencia
del Agua
y del Fuego
desde Antigua,
sin la mancha morada
de Atitlán,
sin oler el copal
quemándose el las gradas
de Chichicastenango
aquel domingo de colores,
tejidos,
rostros herméticos
y polvo
y tropezones.
Se desliza el taxi
en el asfalto.
Me conduce con ritmo
de cornetas,
mariachis
cantinfladas,
costras de revolución.
Recorro los barrios de adobe,
el neón de Reforma
y de Madero.
Los cambios me confunden.
De la larga jornada
me quedan los adioses:
adiós a Maitencillo,
a la playa de noche;

I swallow Guatemala without tasting,
without the brooding presence of the Agua
and the Fuego looming over Antigua,
without the cobalt stain of Atitlan,
without smelling copal
smoldering on the steps of Chichicastenango.
On that colorful Sunday of rebozos,
secret faces and dust.
The taxi glides over asphalt.
It carries me to the rhythm
of trumpets, mariachis, *Cantinfladas*
and to the scars of revolution.
I walk through the clay *barrios*
the neon signs of Reforma and Madero.
The changes hurl me through
the long trajectory
where only my good-byes will remain.
Good-bye to Maitencillo,
the beach at night,

a las calles de Mérida,
fosforescentes;
a Tito castigándose las cejas;
a la nieve arenosa en Farellones—
los cóndores
Manuel—,
a las fatigosas discusiones con María Elena;
a Miquel
y su oscura resignación;
al jardín botánico en otoño;
a los tangos de Idea
y su conjunto inexistente;
a las velas titilando
en Botafogo;
al cursi carnaval
en 18 de julio
con Luz
y Mario
y confetti.
"Me he puesto a teclearte estas líneas
mientras pasan los tanques rumbo a Buenos Aires",
me escriba Roa.
"No veo pasar a los mastodontes de hierro,
pero los oigo avanzar, rechinando.
¿Te acuerdas de lo que hablabamos con Bud, contigo,
oyéndonos los pensamientos, queriendo para nuestra América
así en singular, un destino que no nos hiciera avergonzar?"
Adiós Roa
y Zoraida
y Sebastián
y Manolo
y Lucho
y Pueyrredón.

to the phosphorescent streets of Mérida.
To Tito, pulling at his eyebrow,
to the sandy snows at Farellones,
the condors,
Manuel—
to the tiresome arguments with Maria Elena;
to Miguel in his resignation;
to the botanical gardens in autumn;
to Idea's tangos and her fantasy orchestra;
to the candles fluttering in Botafogo
to the gaudy carnival
along 18 of July
with Luz and Mario and confetti.
From Roa,
"I write these lines
while the tanks roll by to Buenos Aires.
I do not watch, but I hear their screeching.
Remember what we talked about
with Bud and you
attentive to our thoughts:
for our America a destiny
that would not fill us with shame?"
Good-bye Roa
and Zoraida
and Sebastián
and Manolo
and Lucho
and Pueyrredón.

NOTES

"Santa Ana in the Dark"

Estelí is a small town in Nicaragua, the birthplace of Claribel Alegría.
Ricardo is Claribel's uncle, who opened a progressive school.
José Angel was a *campesino* child adopted by the Alegría family.

"Sorrow"

Cuando sepas . . . are the words of Roque Dalton, a Salvadoran poet killed in 1975.
Victor Jara was a Chilean folksinger killed by the security forces in 1973 in the stadium of Santiago.
Listos para la muerte . . . is attributed to Ernesto "Che" Guevara, Argentine-born revolutionary killed in Bolivia in 1968.
Verde que . . . is from "Romances Somnambulo" by the Spanish poet Federico Garcia Lorca.
El crimen fue en Granada . . . is attributed by Claribel Alegría to the Spanish poet Antonio Machado.
La Fuente Grande is a spring located eleven kilometers from Granada in Andalusia.
Cuantos siglos . . . is from "Andaluces de Jaen" by the Spanish poet Miguel Hernandez.
Guayabo is a sweet fruit.
Mate is an herb tea.
Nothing matters . . . is from a tango sung by Tiepolo.
Me morire . . . is from the poem "Piedra negra sobre una piedra blanca" by the Guatemalan poet Cesar Vallejo, in which he prophesies his own death.
Sandino refers to Cesar Augusto Sandino, who led insurgent Nicaraguan forces against the U. S. Marine occupation of Nicaragua during the 1920s and 1930s.
Andaluces de Jaen . . . is from the poem "Andaluces de Jaen" by Miguel Hernandez.
Violeta refers to Violeta Parra, a Chilean folksinger.
The shepherd poet is a reference to Miguel Hernandez.

"My Good-byes"

Escazu, Mombo, et al., are the names of volcanos in Central America.
Sihuatehuacán is the Indian name for the valley of Santa Ana; it is translated as the valley of beautiful women (or witches).
Agua and Fuego are two volcanos in Guatemala.

NOTES

Antigua is a city of Guatemala.
Atitlán is a lake in the highlands of Guatemala.
Roa is a reference to Paraguayan novelist Augusto Roa Bastos.
Zoraida et al., are the names of friends.
18 of July is a street name.

"Flowers from the Volcano"

Chacmol is the Mayan god of thunder and lightning and the inventor of agriculture. A chacmol is also a figurine of stone in a supine position with an impression in or stone bowl on the belly, where the smoking hearts of sacrificial victims were dropped.
"Siete de Junio" is a popular song of unknown origin sung in El Salvador during the earthquake of 1917.
Tlaloc is another name for the Mayan god of thunder and lightning.

BIOGRAPHICAL NOTES

Claribel Alegría was born in Estelí, Nicaragua in 1924, but she considers herself Salvadoran because she went to live in El Salvador when she was a year old. She came to the United States in 1943 and earned her B.A. from George Washington University. She married Darwin J. Flakoll in 1947. They now live in Deya, Mallorca. Her books of poetry include *Anillo de Silencio, Suite, Vigilias, Acuario, Huesped de mi Tiempo, Via Unica, Aprendizaje, Pagare a cobrar y otras poemas, Raices,* and *Sobrevivo*. A selected poems, *Suma y sigue (antologia),* appeared from Visor Madrid in 1981 and her translations of North American poets, *Nuevas voces de Norteamerica,* appeared from Plaza & Janes, S.A., the same year. In 1978, Claribel Alegría was awarded the Casa de las Americas Prize in Havana, Cuba.

Carolyn Forché was born in 1950 in Detroit. Her first book of poems, *Gathering the Tribes,* won the Yale Series of Younger Poets Award in 1975. Between 1978 and 1980 she worked as a journalist and human rights investigator in El Salvador. In 1981 she received the di Castagnola Award from the Poetry Society of America for the working manuscript of her second book of poems. When *The Country Between Us* appeared from the Copper Canyon Press and Harper & Row, Publishers, Inc., in 1982, the Academy of American Poets awarded it their Lamont Selection. She has held Guggenheim and National Endowment for the Arts fellowships and is currently living in Charlottesville, Virginia.

PITT POETRY SERIES

Ed Ochester, General Editor

Dannie Abse, *Collected Poems*

Claribel Alegría, *Flowers from the Volcano*

Jon Anderson, *Death and Friends*

Jon Anderson, *In Sepia*

Jon Anderson, *Looking for Jonathan*

John Balaban, *After Our War*

Michael Benedikt, *The Badminton at Great Barrington; Or, Gustave Mahler & the Chattanooga Choo-Choo*

Michael Burkard, *Ruby for Grief*

Kathy Callaway, *Heart of the Garfish*

Siv Cedering, *Letters from the Floating World*

Lorna Dee Cervantes, *Emplumada*

Robert Coles, *A Festering Sweetness: Poems of American People*

Leo Connellan, *First Selected Poems*

Kate Daniels, *The White Wave*

Norman Dubie, *Alehouse Sonnets*

Stuart Dybek, *Brass Knuckles*

Odysseus Elytis, *The Axion Esti*

John Engels, *Blood Mountain*

Brendan Galvin, *The Minutes No One Owns*

Brendan Galvin, *No Time for Good Reasons*

Gary Gildner, *Blue Like the Heavens: New & Selected Poems*

Gary Gildner, *Digging for Indians*

Gary Gildner, *First Practice*

Gary Gildner, *Nails*

Gary Gildner, *The Runner*

Bruce Guernsey, *January Thaw*

Mark Halperin, *Backroads*

Michael S. Harper, *Song: I Want a Witness*

John Hart, *The Climbers*

Gwen Head, *Special Effects*

Gwen Head, *The Ten Thousandth Night*

Milne Holton and Graham W. Reid, eds., *Reading the Ashes: An Anthology of the Poetry of Modern Macedonia*

Milne Holton and Paul Vangelisti, eds., *The New Polish Poetry: A Bilingual Collection*

David Huddle, *Paper Boy*

Lawrence Joseph, *Shouting at No One*

Shirley Kaufman, *The Floor Keeps Turning*

Shirley Kaufman, *From One Life to Another*

Shirley Kaufman, *Gold Country*
Ted Kooser, *One World at a Time*
Ted Kooser, *Sure Signs: New and Selected Poems*
Larry Levis, *Winter Stars*
Larry Levis, *Wrecking Crew*
Robert Louthan, *Living in Code*
Tom Lowenstein, tr., *Eskimo Poems from Canada and Greenland*
Archibald MacLeish, *The Great American Fourth of July Parade*
Peter Meinke, *Trying to Surprise God*
Judith Minty, *In the Presence of Mothers*
Carol Muske, *Camouflage*
Carol Muske, *Wyndmere*
Leonard Nathan, *Dear Blood*
Leonard Nathan, *Holding Patterns*
Kathleen Norris, *The Middle of the World*
Sharon Olds, *Satan Says*
Greg Pape, *Black Branches*
Greg Pape, *Border Crossings*
Thomas Rabbitt, *Exile*
James Reiss, *Express*
Ed Roberson, *Etai-Eken*
Eugene Ruggles, *The Lifeguard in the Snow*
Dennis Scott, *Uncle Time*
Herbert Scott, *Groceries*
Richard Shelton, *Of All the Dirty Words*
Richard Shelton, *Selected Poems, 1969-1981*
Richard Shelton, *You Can't Have Everything*
Gary Soto, *Black Hair*
Gary Soto, *The Elements of San Joaquin*
Gary Soto, *The Tale of Sunlight*
Gary Soto, *Where Sparrows Work Hard*
Tomas Tranströmer, *Windows & Stones: Selected Poems*
Chase Twichell, *Northern Spy*
Constance Urdang, *The Lone Woman and Others*
Constance Urdang, *Only the World*
Ronald Wallace, *Tunes for Bears to Dance To*
Cary Waterman, *The Salamander Migration and Other Poems*
Bruce Weigl, *A Romance*
David P. Young, *The Names of a Hare in English*
Paul Zimmer, *Family Reunion: Selected and New Poems*